This book belongs to

_____

Chloe Kim

By Mary Nhin

Illustrated By
Yuliia Zolotova

Hi, I'm Chloe Kim.

I was born on Easter Sunday.
And I started snowboarding
when I was four years old.

Actually, my dad and I learned how to snowboard together at a snowboarding resort nearby our home in California.

Even though my dad didn't really know much about snowboarding, he enjoyed the sport and had an engineering background.

He nurtured my love for snowboarding and tried to come up with new ways to help me improve. My dad was my very first coach!

Even as a young girl, my dad said I rode fearlessly, always eager to try again after every fall.

We didn't know much about protection, so my dad used to cut up my mom's yoga mats and put them in my pants so it wouldn't hurt as much when I fell.

He used to have me train my flips and tricks on our trampoline in the backyard of our home.

My dad also encouraged me to ride "switch," which meant leading with my left leg forward. At first, it felt really weird, but this eventually helped to develop both sides of my body and made it easier for me to do difficult tricks!

When I turned six, I began competing on the local snowboarding team. Even though, it was hard work, I remember having so much fun with the other kids.

One time at a competition, my dad forgot to book a hotel, so we ended up staying the night in our car.

I continued to work hard and trained in Geneva, Switzerland. And I even won the junior nationals!

When I was around nine or ten, I fell in love with the sport and knew I wanted to do this for the rest of my life. So when I returned to California to train at Mammoth Mountain, that's exactly what I told my mom and dad.

Do you know what they said?

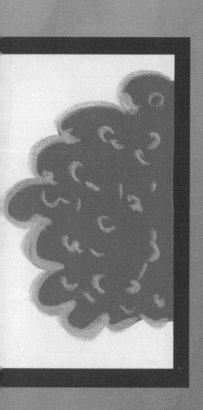

My father announced he was going to give up his job and stop working so he could take me to all my sporting events. My parents really believed in me!

In 2013, I officially joined the U.S. snowboarding team. On the snow, I loved to push boundaries by doing gravity-defying twists and turns.

I earned enough points to qualify for the Sochi Olympics, but I couldn't compete because I wasn't old enough.

Finally, when I was 17, I was able to compete in the 2018 Olympics. That year, I won the gold medal, becoming the youngest to accomplish this feat.

Training and competing so much meant that I had to miss out on regular teenage stuff like going to dances.

The sacrifice was worth it, though. I became the first snowboarder who held titles from four major events.

Toyota would love for you to become an ambassador, Chloe!

We'd love to sponsor you, Chloe!

Samsung needs you, Chloe!

Chloe is one of the best switch riders in the snowboarding world.

It's not like I was just dropped onto a snowboard and I was able to go 15 feet into the air. There was a lot of hard work that came with it. That's something that people don't really notice sometimes and the amount of sacrifice my family made.

Timeline

2014 – Chloe earns a silver medal in superpipe
in Winter X Games

2015 – Chloe earns a gold medal in superpipe in
Winter X Games

2016 – Chloe becomes first person to win two
gold medals in Winter X Games, and first
person to win back to back gold medals.

2016 – Chloe becomes first person to land back
to back 1080 spins at Grand Prix

2018 – Chloe wins her first Olympic Gold Medal
in the Women's Halfpipe

minimovers.tv

 @marynhin   @GrowGrit
#minimoversandshakers

 Mary Nhin   Ninja Life Hacks

 Ninja Life Hacks

 @ninjalifehacks.tv